Minimalistic Living
2021

Table of Contents

Conclusion

Introduction

Living in today's society can be stressful. We have a million things on our to-do list, and we're always running from one task to anther, never really finishing one thing before we start another. All of this leads to stress, feelings of being overwhelmed, anxiety, and even depression. These are not roads to go down voluntarily. We need to find ways to simplify life, whilst still enjoying the same perks. Isn't life meant to be enjoyed, to be full of wonderful experiences and relationships which bring joy ? Today's society has a habit doing the opposite in so many ways.

This book is about something called minimalism. Before you begin to panic and think that you need to throw out all your worldly belongings, take a moment to relax because that's actually not what this concept is about. Minimalism is as much a mindset as it is about decluttering. You will declutter physically, for sure, but you will also need to examine what you really need in life to be happy. The fact that you have picked up this book is a sign that you are searching for something more, perhaps the desire to fill a gap, or maybe you're tired of feeling like you've always been striving for something impossible. If that is the case, minimalism is something which can help you get the answer and experience it first hand.

Much of the time we place a huge amount of importance on 'things'. For instance, we're always striving to have the latest cell phone, the most up to date technology, but do we really need it? If you need it for work then that makes sense but if you simply want it, that's something else altogether. Perhaps you also want this item because your friend or colleague has it, and you want to be 'level' with them. But who actually decides that owning a particular product makes you better than someone else that doesn't ?

Minimalism teaches us that we don't need physical things to be happy, and that true contentment is actually found within ourselves, the things we hold dear in life and the relationships we have. When you achieve this minimalist state of mind, you'll actually realise that true happiness is very rare, and that the only way to truly get to that point is by searching deep within.

Throughout this book, we're going to talk in much more detail about what minimalism is, the cultural aspects and the history, and we're going to give plenty of practical advice on how to achieve a minimalistic lifestyle. By the end of the book, you should be ready and raring to change the way you think and live, eager to grab the benefits of total contentment and happiness. There is a certain amount of preparation to be done, and a good amount of decluttering in the physical space, but also in your mind. Every single step of this process is necessary, and more than worth your time and effort.

Enough procrastination, it's time to learn what minimalism is, and start our new journey toward personal liberation and contentment. Let's get started!

Chapter 1: Introduction to Minimalism

This first chapter is going to give you the basic principles and ideas of what minimalism is and where it came from. When you have the basic information, you can start your journey on the best possible footing.

Many people confuse the term 'minimalism' with interior decoration or something similar but it's more than just deciding not to have a lot of furniture in your living room! Minimalism in so many ways is about an intention. You are telling yourself that you are going to live your best life with only the things that you really need. You're not going to clutter your life or space with the things that aren't necessary for your health or wellbeing, and instead, you're going to concentrate on necessities.

Let's break it down a little further.

What is Minimalism?

Minimalism is an intention and a promise to yourself, but it comes from within and has nothing to do with outside influences. By choosing a minimalistic lifestyle, you are opting to only own or have the things which you need in your life, which bring you value, and to throw out or cast away anything which causes a distraction. It is a way of thinking and a core value which brings improvements to your entire life.

For instance, minimalism helps you see the world differently, and it helps you to value things so much more as a result.

This isn't to say that you can't own nice things, of course, you can, but you would question whether or not you really need them, before deciding to make that purchase. This also comes down to the relationships in your life. You would not clutter your life with friendships that aren't necessary, and instead, you would stick to nurturing connections which bring something useful and meaningful.

By clearing out your life in this way, both physically and mentally, you are freeing up space in your brain for value and meaning. It isn't about needing to own the latest gadget or the most up to date label of jeans, it's about knowing that what you have is what you need without having to copy or duplicate someone else.

The most important thing to realise about minimalism is that it comes from within and it is not something which can be chosen without intention. A person who begins to live a minimalistic lifestyle needs to make the choice with intention, and they need to know why they're doing it. It's so easy to be seduced by what we think we need, or by a desire to live up to standards set by other people, such as celebrities, magazines and the media. But you will need the strength of character to resist all of that and we will learn in following chapters how exactly do that.

Most of us don't live minimalistic lifestyles these days. We might think we do to some degree, but we're so easily attracted to physical things and ownership that it takes a real change of mindset to achieve the minimalistic standard. The end result of achieving minimalism is contentment, an easier life and a happier mind.

To sum up, minimalism is:

- Living life with just the things you need

- Asking yourself whether you really need something or you just want it

- An intention and spoken vow that you will not clutter your life with the things that hold no meaning in your life and for your higher self

- Not only about physical goods to own, but also about relationships and friendships in life

- A way to achieve total contentment and happiness

- A mindset and a way of life, not something which can be dibbed in and out of

-

Why People Practice Minimalism

You might wonder why people bother practising minimalism when there are so many fancy goods to own. Let's face it, it's nice to buy the latest iPhone and have time to sit and play with it, but what you should ask yourself is what value it brings to your life. Sure, it takes great photographs and you can play games on it whenever you please, but does that make you truly happy ? Does it make your life worthwhile ? Does it create a sense of contentment ? Be honest with yourself when trying to find answers to these questions. If you feel in the depths of your soul that upgrading your phone to the next version will bring you lasting happiness then go for it. But it turns out that for most people on this planet, the answer to whether materialistic pursuits bring them lasting happiness is is - Not really, not in the long-run at least.

People choose to practice minimalism because they're fed up of feeling like they're always trying to achieve something and never actually gaining the benefits. For instance, in a short while, we're going to talk about the modern need to always match standards, e.g. Instagram influencers and their power over society. If we're always trying to reach an unspoken standard, e.g. have a certain look, or own a certain type of phone, it's never going to be enough. Why? Because these standards and trends are always changing. Life never stands still. You might have the latest phone for, say, six months. Then a new version comes onto the market and yours is outdated. It's exhausting! You're chasing an ideal that will never be true.

On the other hand, minimalism is not about that constant hamster wheel, you're still, you're static, and you're happy where you are. You have what you need to live your life and you're content. Never underestimate how fantastic being content feels !

People choose to live a minimalistic lifestyle because they no longer want to chase an unrealistic ideal, they don't want to try and 'keep up with the Kardashians' anymore, and they're tired of nothing ever being enough. When you live in a minimalistic way, everything is enough, and that's the whole point.

Another reason why someone might decide to go down the minimalist route is stress. For many of us, the daily life is always so busy and full of running around from one thing to another. It becomes overwhelming, tiring, and depressing. In some cases, you hit a wall, and you can no longer do it. You start to ask yourself if it's all worth it, and you want to make changes - right now. Choosing the minimalist way is the single best way to combat stress and choose a quieter, more peaceful life.

Look at it this way - when you're out with your partner or a close friend, do you become annoyed at them because they always seem to be on their phone? You've come out to eat a meal together and spend quality time, but he or she is messaging someone far away, or checking the latest news online, perhaps scrolling through Instagram. This is such a common occurrence these days. We lose sight of the relationships which are right in front of us, because we're too busy living in a digital world, one that doesn't actually exist. We don't see the beauty of the things around us because we're too busy staring at a small piece of plastic which connects us to what we think is the 'world'. If only the millennials could understand that it's not the world, it's a virtual reality that they're choosing to plug into.

When you choose to be a minimalist, you give yourself the power to open your eyes to the wonder of nature, the beauty all around you, and you can dedicate time to the important relationships in your life. Slow down, smell the daisies!

Origins & Historical References of Minimalist Living

Minimalism has been practised throughout history and actually dates back centuries. Whilst it might not have had a specific name or been a real lifestyle choice, it was simply something which was done in an unspoken manner. Minimalism was much easier back in the day because there weren't as many temptations and certainly not as much emphasis on ownership.

Religious groups in particular, e.g. Buddhists, have long had a history of avoiding or renouncing ownership, in order to become more focused or to gain wisdom. You could even go as far as to think about Buddhist monks or even nuns in the Catholic religion. This is a form of minimalism. Whilst you don't have to go that far if you don't want to, the idea is the same - living with what you need and doing more with it, e.g. gaining wisdom and a more peaceful way of life. You could also adopt the minimalism idea into the Islamic holy month of Ramadan. During this time, Muslims fast during the hours of sunrise to sunset, in order to gain wisdom and a greater sense of clarity. The background idea is the same - you do not need material 'things' in order to gain wisdom or happiness.

Minimalism began to seep its way into the home decoration world sometime in the '70s, becoming trendy to have less in the home, to create a greater space. Again, the idea is the same, even if the type of minimalism we're talking about is more about the mind than the household.

Why Minimalism is so Crucial in The Modern Age

We should point out that minimalism is not about going without. It isn't about denying yourself simple pleasures in life, but it is about reassessing what you consider those pleasure to be. For instance, if you think a simple pleasure is to get a brand new computer, you need to think more critically! Remember, minimalism helps us understand the value of things, so once you have been in this lifestyle for a longer time, you'll begin to see things for what they are and enjoy them for their real value. It's a wonderful feeling to really feel joy in every small thing.

A little earlier we touched upon the modern society's obsessions and why material ownership has run riot. These days, modern culture has decided that happiness lies in owning things, and in having the latest things and more of them. Basically, the more the better, and this somehow equates to power, happiness, and wellness. We are told that happiness lies in the Apple Store or in a shopping mall. Happiness does not lie in either of those places, it lies within you.

We are also always trying to keep up with everyone around us. For instance, if someone you admire owns a new pair of sneakers, you'll be tempted to buy the same ones, because that somehow makes you as good as them. There is nothing bad about you, and you are already as good as them, a pair of sneakers makes no difference! Minimalism, in this case, helps you to become a stronger, more confident person because you're not attempting to compare yourself to others and always seeming to come up short. Consider Instagram influencers for instance - these people are telling us we need to

own this product or that product and it will make us beautiful and healthy. Will it really? Deep down we know that person is being paid to market that product and make us believe what they're saying.

Minimalism is so vitally important in the modern day because we are constantly being bombarded with messages via every medium of communication possible. Life isn't about comparisons, it isn't about keeping up with the Jones, the Kardashians, or anyone else. It's about finding value in the smaller things that truly bring us happiness and joy. Escaping the trap of consumerism and daring to seek out happiness and contentment elsewhere can bring huge rewards. Fortune favors the bold. So you should start looking away from your mobile phone or laptop and towards other things (nature, your own experiences, interpersonal relationships etc).

What Will Happen if You Prioritise Materialism Over Minimalism ?

In the long run, if you choose to prioritise materialism over minimalism, you will struggle to be happy. It's that simple. History is full of stories of men and women who chased external entities like gold, empires, power, sex, food, pleasure only to witness the emptiness that faced them on the other side of this pursuit.

You cannot find happiness in something you have purchased. You might feel a rush for a short while, and you might feel pride at owning something so new and shiny, but it will fade and you'll be left with a huge gaping hole once more. This might lead you to try and purchase something else, to get the same rush. Do you see how materialism can lead to addiction for example to shopping?

There is a very real danger for today's generation with addiction and accumulating physical things as opposed to seeking out deeper experiences and meaningful connections.

There are a few outcomes to favouring materialism in your life:

• You will never achieve contentment and happiness

• You will live life in a constant hamster wheel, always trying to reach a goal that is never static, always moving

• You will lack confidence because your self-worth is linked so drastically to ownership

- You run the risk of developing an addiction or dependence on buying new things

- Your financial stability may be at risk as a result

That doesn't paint the greatest pictures, does it? In the upcoming few chapters we will look closer into the root cause of this issue and how we can fix it at the core.

What We Have Learnt in This Chapter

In this chapter, we have learnt what minimalism is and why it is such a beneficial way of life. We have defined it as best as we can and we have talked about why it is so important to become more minimal in our way of thinking in this busy day and age.

Remember, minimalism isn't about never owning anything, and it's not about treating yourself like a slave. Minimalism is about being more aware and questioning whether you really need something versus whether you want it. If you need something in your life, by all means, purchase it. If you just want something, it's time to ask yourself what that product can give you which your relationships and inner happiness can't.

Minimalism is about moving away from consumerism, and about making a choice to avoid materialism. You do not need more 'stuff' to make you happy, and once you realise that you will quickly begin to enjoy a happier, more content life.

This chapter is designed to give you the basics, to help you understand the crux of what we're going to go on and explore in more detail in our upcoming chapters. Make sure you understand the basic points in this chapter that form the basis for the rest of our conversations.

Chapter 2: The Hoarding Crisis - Why Modern Society is Focused on Accumulating Material Possessions

We have to explore the idea of hoarding and materialism a lot more in order to truly understand why minimalism is a far greater option. Only when something clicks in your mind, when you really 'get it' can you choose a better option.

Minimalism is an intention, remember. It is something you need to live your life by. You can't half understand it, because your mind will always be in conflict. You have to completely understand it and you have to know that your spirit is in agreement. Only then can you live the life with contentment. Otherwise, you're going to think that you're right, but a voice in your head is going to be saying 'go on, buy it'. You'll always be in conflict and having a war with yourself. There's no fun in that.

By having the full understanding, you'll be able to choose the minimalistic way of life for the right reasons.

So, what is hoarding?

There are two sides to hoarding. One is keeping things and refusing to throw them away because you might need them 'one day', and the other is buying things for the sake of it. Hoarding and shopping addictions are quite closely linked.

You might have a cupboard full of things that you never use, but you refuse to throw them away or donate them to a charity because what if you suddenly need them one day? What if you suddenly wake up on a Thursday morning and need the four vases you have sitting in a cupboard? It's highly unlikely you will ever need those vases but your brain tricks you into thinking that your life will somehow be less meaningful if they are no longer sat in the cupboard.

That is the mindset of a hoarder.

There is nobody in the world who doesn't hoard to some degree when they are not firmly in the minimalistic lifestyle. Everyone who doesn't live the minimalist way hoards a certain amount, and it is usually through bulk buying or buying things that you really don't need.

Why People Become Addicted to Shopping And Accumulating Possessions

Do you consider yourself a shopaholic? Think about it carefully. Becoming addicted to shopping and owning things is a serious condition. Just like becoming addicted to drugs, smoking, alcohol, becoming addicted to purchasing things and accumulating possessions is about dependency.

A person who is addicted to shopping gets a high from the process. They find joy in purchasing something new and taking it home. When they swipe their card and the product goes into a carrier bag to be carried home, they feel on top of the world, and it's a chemical high which can be super-addictive. Of course, as with most highs, it diminishes very quickly, and you're left needing another hit in order to feel that good again.

Between the highs come the lows. You start to realise that you've spent too much money, and you might start hiding credit card bills, or placing your purchases under the bed so that your partner doesn't see them and starts questioning you on why you needed another pair of shoes, another phone, another whatever. Both men and women are equally affected by an addiction to accumulating possessions and shopping. This is not a gender thing, although we tend to focus more on women wanting to buy clothes and shoes; men are equally as prone to purchasing unwanted things in a controllable manner, an addictive manner.

So, why do people become addicted to shopping and accumulating items?

For the same reason that perhaps someone becomes addicted to alcohol or binge eating - the high is so delicious. Once it becomes a continuous cycle, addiction is damaging in so many levels.

Maybe you don't consider yourself to have an addiction, but if you are always drawn to purchasing things and you can't stop yourself, you need to question why you're doing it.

Are you doing it because you're trying to keep up with someone? Are you comparing yourself to someone and purchasing the same items as them in an attempt to 'copy' them or somehow compete? Modern society has become so addicted to 'one-upping' one another that purchasing unneeded items has become almost second nature for so many.

Emotional Causes For Embracing Materialism

Of course, there is a myriad of reasons why someone might get so attracted to materialism, but most of them are emotional. A few potential reasons include:

- A lack of self-confidence and discipline

- Trying to recover from one addiction, and reframing it into another

- Feeling lack in some way, e.g. comparisons to other people and coming up short in your own mind

- Distraction techniques - many people develop an addiction when they are trying not to deal with another issue in their lives, e.g. depression, guilt, or unresolved anger

- Shopping once more as a way of trying to reduce the guilt of the last shopping spree

Materialism does not lead to happiness and it does nothing for confidence. Choosing material things over more deeper connections leads to disconnections in so many areas of life. By addressing the emotional problem at hand, and not trying to avoid it, a person can get away from the grips of consumerism and materialism, but minimalism is a sure fire answer to this problem.

There are a few different types of shopaholics we should mention:

- Emotional shoppers - Those who want to purchase new things because they are feeling distressed emotionally

- Shoppers who are looking for the perfect item - This is a never-ending cycle

- Shoppers who want people to think they're somehow superior - This is a confidence issue, as wanting someone to have a specific view of you is a sign of very low self-worth

- Compulsive shoppers who want to find bargains - This type of shopper is always looking for cut-price items, but in reality, these are not bargains, because you don't need them!

- Cyclic shoppers - These shoppers buy things and take them back, simply to get the hit of purchasing something

Regardless of the type of shopaholic, there is a deep-seated need which is not being addressed, and in order to solve it, a certain amount of soul searching, personal development or even professional help may be necessary.

What We Have Learnt in This Chapter

This chapter has explored the modern day problem of materialism and shopping addictions in greater detail. It is far easier to develop a shopping problem these days than it has ever been before. There is so much focus on owning things and being the one with the flashiest item, the newest piece of technology, that overspending and developing a habit can become all too easy.

In order to escape the grips of materialism, it's vital to understand the reason for needing to own these things in the first place. What are you lacking? Do you feel that you're not good enough? What exactly is driving your need to purchase something?

Once you've understood the reason for your attraction towards hoarding, you can get a birds-eye view of your life circumstances. And that will lead to much better decisions in the journey towards creating a life of fulfillment. Minimalism is the ideal antidote to today's problem of materialism.

Chapter 3: The Top Five Benefits of a Minimalist Lifestyle

You're not going to embrace the minimalist lifestyle unless you understand the benefits. After all, we don't do anything unless there is something in it for us, right? That is exactly why, in this chapter, we are going to explore the numerous benefits we get to see for ourselves when we decide to live a minimal life.

The great thing about living this kind of lifestyle is that the benefits are very rewarding, and even though we are only going to mention the top five in this chapter, there are far more that you'll witness in your own journey. As with anything in life, you get out of it what you put into it. So if you give your all to adopting the minimalistic lifestyle, you will find that the rewards are far greater. You will be able to feel more of a difference compared to if you are simply half in and half out.

The top five benefits of a minimalist lifestyle are:

- You create space for what is really important
- A clearer head that is not constantly filled with distractions
- Time and attention to focus on health, hobbies, and learning
- Far less priority for material possessions and competition
- A greater sense of happiness, confidence and contentment

Let's explore each one in a little more detail.

Space For What is Really Important

By getting rid of everything in your life that you don't really need, you are creating a lot of new space. This is both physical and mental space. By doing this, you are giving yourself the opportunity to explore what is really important in life.

A little earlier we mentioned the fact that most people spend too much time on their phones and don't really take stock of what is going on around them. This is a huge problem in today's society. By turning to the minimalist lifestyle, you are understanding what is important in life, and realising that it isn't about having the latest model of phone, or wearing the latest fashion. These things do not bring true happiness, they only bring a quick 'hit' of happiness which fades just as quickly as it arrived.

Spending time with loved ones, learning new things, finding out what you really want in life, these are the most important things to understand. The clarity of mind that you get by clearing out your physical space is almost always underrated. It will give you the time and the opportunity to explore things in greater detail.

Once you've done it, you'll realise how ridiculous materialism really is! Does owning the latest computer bring us closer to our siblings? No! It actually takes us further away. Does owning the most up to date brand of sneakers make us a better friend to someone we've known for years? Not at all. In our attempt to become someone "cool " or "worthy ", we tend to isolate our closest friends and family. Our thirst for more is what blinds us to what already is.

The most important things in life can't be bought or hoarded and this is something which minimalism will teach you. Remember, the people in our lives will not be there forever, and when the time comes for us to bid them goodbye (as upsetting a thought as that is), you'll wish you had given more time to the simple things, rather than focusing all your attention onto owning the latest tech or fashion items.

A Clearer Head

Minimalism helps to clear the mind in many ways. Firstly, it's about the physical once more. The less 'stuff' you have sitting around, the clearer you will feel. For instance, when you are at work, if you work within a desk area, do you find it easy to work when there are countless pieces of paper, folders, files, and other pieces of junk lying around? No! You can't move for things and they're taking up important space which you need for the job at hand. This is exactly the same process in your brain. The more clutter you have around you, the harder it is to focus.

There is a reason that many workplaces are streamlining their workstations - because many studies have shown that tidy desks create a tidy mind and increase productivity as a result. You can adopt the same way of thinking to any part of your life. For instance, if your car is constantly messy, full of junk, will you enjoy driving in it? It won't be the same, that's for sure. On the other hand, if you clear everything out, throw away the junk and keep it tidy, you'll enjoy your journeys and you'll be more proud of your vehicle.

Constantly trying to keep up with everyone by owning the latest gadgets and trends creates a cluttered mind also. You're never satisfied, you're never in the moment, and you're always thinking ahead, never really content with where you are. Minimalism will teach you that a clear and tidy space will give you a clearer mind and therefore you can use that to reach your full potential in life. You will have a better basis on which to build your career, explore your likes and dislikes, etc.

Time and Space to Focus on Health, Hobbies, and Learning

A clearer headspace also gives you the time you need to focus on other things in life, e.g. your health, your hobbies, and lifelong learning. Most of us become so stuck on materialism that it takes over everything else in life. Is owning material items more important than your health? Is owning material items more important than enjoying your spare time? Is it more important than learning new skills which could catapult your life to the next level?

By clearing out your mind and your physical space, you are creating time, something which most of us don't have enough of. You can find the things you need, you can move around much more freely, and your mind isn't cluttered. This means that you can focus on whatever it is that you want to focus on, without anything else getting in the way.

You will feel lighter on your feet and that will directly affect your health. You won't be dumbed down by the need to own, and you won't be as stressed out as a result. Remember, owning material goods is an expensive business, and money worries can become so serious that they create a world of stress and anxiety. None of that is positive.

When you feel less stressed and healthier on the inside, you are more likely to think about effective and fun ways to fill your time. You can create new hobbies, perhaps walking, something active, or something creative, and you can learn new things too. You'll have the time and space to think about your life and what you want from it, and if that means going back to school and learning a language or something new altogether, go for it! Minimalism will give you the confidence to go for what you want because you have realised what is truly important in life.

Less Focus on Material Possessions And Competition

When you focus on always being ahead of everyone else, e.g. trying to be the one with the latest gadget, for instance, you'll always be stressed and you'll never be still. As we mentioned earlier in our book, technology and fashions move at such an alarming rate, it's impossible to always be the one with the best stuff. A phone is never the latest model for long! This means that you're constantly on the lookout for the latest thing, you're always trying to have the cash to actually purchase these things, many of which are extremely expensive.

Being in competition with everyone else, i.e. wanting to be the one who has the latest things, is exhausting. It doesn't allow you to form meaningful relationships with anyone. How can you be a true friend to someone if you're always striving to prove that you're better than them?

Having less focus on owning material possessions and competing to be the best will allow you to be a better friend, a better family member, and a better everything to someone else. You're focused on them as a person, and not always trying to be the better one out of the two of you. Materialism is a really negative trait, and whilst it is never intended to be, it can actually ruin relationships and cause huge yawning gaps between people who were once close.

A Greater Sense of Happiness, Confidence, and Contentment

All of this adds up to one thing - happiness. When you feel lighter, you feel healthier, you're focused on the things you enjoy, and you have meaningful relationships with those around you then how can you be unhappy? You'll be more content because you are happy with what you have, you don't need to always be striving for something which you're never going to achieve or own, and you'll feel more confident in yourself as a result.

Most of us don't know what true happiness really feels like. We think we do, but we often think that happiness is when our new cellphone has been delivered from the phone company and we have a full day to play with it. That's not happiness at its deepest level, that's just a quick hit of adrenaline from owning something new. The shine quickly fades and we're looking for the next thing we can own. The highs and lows which come from this do not equate to happiness, they equate to drama and stress.

Feeling at ease with everything and not particularly needing to strive for anything that you can't reach is a truly magnificent feeling, and it can be achieved by adopting a minimalist lifestyle. The confidence which comes from feeling content and happy will actually be a major turning point in your life. When you're confident, you seek out opportunities for change, because your newly positive attitude attracts them. When they come, you're more likely to take them, and who knows where that could lead!

For instance, perhaps a promotion opportunity occurs at work and you want to go for it, but you're so stressed out living the materialistic lifestyle, running from one thing to another and never really grabbing what you want, that you don't have the confidence or sense of self-worth to go for it. On the other hand, someone who is content and happy with their lot will have the mindset of 'what have I got to lose?'. From there, wonderful things happen, usually quite unexpected things.

What We Have Learnt in This Chapter

In this chapter, we have talked about the top five benefits of adopting a minimalist lifestyle. As you will see, they overlap somewhat and one leads into another. Being minimalistic in your approach to life has this effect, and every positive thing leads to another. Happiness has a way of making everything else in your life far more positive as a result.

There are many other benefits of living a minimalist life, such as saving money and being able to put it towards something amazing, such as a travel experience. Avoiding materialism will teach you that the greatest things in life can't be bought per se. Whilst life is expensive in general and we need to pay for most things, it's not about ownership. It's better to pay to go to an amazing place than it is to pay for a new bag or a new pair of shoes. That travel experience will teach you things, 2it will allow you to meet new people, and it will open your eyes to a new culture. That is far more valuable and important than anything you can own.

In our next chapter, we're going to get a little practical, and we're going to talk about how to actually get started with adopting the mindset required for a life of minimalism.

Chapter 4: The Mindset of Minimalist Living

It's time to get practical! Adopting a minimalistic mindset will take practice. Do not worry if you attempt to start this way of thinking but then you have the odd moment of materialism temptation. That is totally normal and something you should actually expect. Remember, this is a completely new way of life and a totally different way of thinking. For that reason, you're bound to have occasional lapses into temptation at first.

What you have to remember however if willpower and the reason you are doing what you're doing. You will know that a minimalist lifestyle will bring you many benefits by this point in the book, so it's important to keep those in mind if you have the odd moment of temptation coming your way. It's normal, don't beat yourself up. What you shouldn't do however is give into it.

Materialism is a strong mindset to have, and you may have been living in the grips of it for a long time already. Breaking free of the need to own and compare will be a mind over matter process for quite a long period of time. Once you break through the other side, however, the results are total calmness and all the many benefits we talked about in our last chapter. Stick with it, the final destination is more than worth it!

In a later chapter, we're going to talk about the practical elements of clearing out and decluttering, but the first step is to harness the power of your mind and stick with it.

The first things you need to do are:

- Reduce the clutter within your house, and most of these are bound to be what are called 'surface items'. If you're guilty of having several ornaments and items of a decorative nature around your home, these need to go. This will declutter your mind to a large degree from the start.

- Start to say 'no'. This means when you see something and you consider buying it for a split second, you say 'no' and walk away. Remind yourself of the benefits and stick with them!

- Clear out the loft space and any boxes. We all have boxes of things we keep which are of sentimental value. The problem is that we consider 'stuff' to be the things we should hold dear when it's actual memories which are more important. You don't have to throw things out, but you can donate them to those who need them more than you or gift them to a family member who likes to hold onto such things. The main point is that you are removing them out of your home and out of your mind, and instead focusing on the things which matter the most - relationships in your life right now and memories of special times gone by.

- Have an 'in and out' guideline. A good way to start with the minimalist lifestyle and to help you get into the swing of it is to have an in and out rule. This means that if you do buy something, you have to throw one thing out as a result. This will make you think twice before you start purchasing items for the sake of it and is a good way to get started on the minimalist road.

These are just a few quick ideas and steps you can start with, to help you begin getting into the swing of the mindset you need to adopt. Remember, at first it might seem hard, but it will pass and you will soon notice that you don't feel as tempted anymore, and you simply don't have interest in the purchasing endeavours that used to attract your attention so much in the past. You'll feel lighter and freer as a result!

How to Adopt Minimalism Into Daily Activities

So, we know that beginning on the minimalist road can be difficult at first and we've given you a few hints and tips on how to begin. What we need to talk about now is how you can actually adopt minimalism into your daily activities and help the habit spread.

The more you practice something, the easier it becomes. It's just the same as going to the gym and lifting weights in order to boost your biceps. The more you flex that muscle, the stronger it becomes. Use the same thought process when you think of your new minimalistic lifestyle - the more you do it, the stronger the mindset becomes, and the more second nature it also becomes.

There are many ways you can adopt the lifestyle into your daily activities, and it will soon become a part of everything you do. It isn't simply about decluttering your home and not buying things when you're tempted, it's about considering what you can do in your life with less.

A few suggestions include:

- Deciding to make a lunch to take to work with you, rather than buying from the local deli

- Choosing to walk to work, rather than taking the bus

- Reorganising your workspace, e.g. decluttering your desk to give you a clearer space in which to work

- Considering borrowing items rather than buying something, e.g. going to the library to rent out a book, rather than going to a book store to buy it new

- Making use of the digital environment, e.g. the Internet, rather than buying items and having more clutter around your home. For instance, download a streaming TV service rather than buying DVDs

- Look for advice on how to do things yourself on YouTube, rather than calling for repair services as soon as something goes slightly wrong

- Look at how you can regenerate or recycle items, rather than throwing them away. For instance, if you have an old chair that is broken, can you fix it and cover it over, to create a brand new look? Can you turn an old pair of jeans into a pair of shorts and wear them in the summer?

- Always think twice before you purchase anything, and ask yourself if you really need it in the first place.

- Dedicate a few hours every day to spending time with people and having conversations in person, rather than on the phone

As you can see, minimalism is as much about the way you think as much as what you do. Asking if you can recycle something before you throw it out, asking yourself whether you really need something before you buy it. These are questions you can start to ask right now, and you'll see quick results too.

What We Have Learnt in This Chapter

This chapter has highlighted how easy it can be to start on the road towards minimalism, but we've also mentioned that at first, you might struggle with temptation. Don't worry if this is the case, it's perfectly normal and nothing to be ashamed of. You have been entrenched in a certain way of thinking for so long, that it's going to take a while to reprogram your mind and think differently. What you shouldn't do is give up, because you will eventually get there!

We've also given you a few examples of how you can implement the minimalistic way of thinking into your daily life. This is by no means an exhaustive list because you can look at any task you're going to do in your day and figure out if you can approach it more minimalistically. It's about being flexible in your thinking and asking questions before you do anything impulsive, e.g. getting a new credit card or shopping online.

In our next chapter, we're going to continue with the practical theme and talk about budgeting. Living a minimalist lifestyle will certainly save you cash, but what you do with the cash you save is just as important. Don't throw it away on meaningless stuff and ruin your efforts by opting to buy something lavish rather it in the right places to make it grow, or spend it on experiences rather than material goods.

Chapter 5: Budgeting Tips For Living a Minimalist Lifestyle

One of the biggest perks of living a minimalist life is that you will save money without even trying. Of course, contentment and happiness are the number one priority, but feeling more financially comfortable and stable is a huge deal and will save you a lot of stress and drama in your journey.

Most people's beliefs about money are very limiting and negative. Money is not inherently a bad thing - we all need it in order to live. This doesn't justify spending it on new clothes, new cars, or new technology whenever we feel like it. It actually means being able to pay our bills, eat, spend time with loved ones, and see the world if we are so inclined. Money isn't for splashing and splurging, it's for things we need. Perhaps as part of your new minimalist way, you could also think about donating some cash every month to charity. That is a personal decision, for sure, but it will give you a warm glow and help you feel more positive overall. This is not philosophical but practical. There is something scientific about the act of giving that triggers the happiness chemicals in our brain.

In this chapter, we're going to talk about budgeting tips which fit in perfectly with your new minimalist lifestyle. These tips will help you save cash, but they will also help you spend it on useful and positive ways, rather than splurging it on material items that you don't actually need. Remember, the whole point of embracing this new lifestyle is to avoid such outcomes, and instead to focus your time and money where it really matters.

Before we get into this list of tips, we need to ascertain one thing - what is a budget?

A budget is a way of living. Just as minimalism is a lifestyle, budgeting is exactly the same. It is living within your means, and not spending cash that you don't have. From that description, you can understand why the two work very well together.

Budgeting means that you look at the money you have every month, make a list of the things you need to pay, and you subtract that total amount. What you have left is your surplus. From this surplus, you need to decide what to do and how to do it, in the most careful and sensible way. Saving is a good option, but as before, perhaps giving a small amount to charity every month is also a good way for you to give something back too.

We'll talk shortly on defining your budget and working out goals, but for now, let's talk about a few tips which can help you adopt the minimalist lifestyle and save cash at the same time.

Investing in Experiences as Opposed to Material Possessions

Material possessions do not last forever, but memories do. For instance, you could buy the latest laptop and it would work wonderfully well for perhaps a couple of years, but eventually, something would break inside it and you would need to replace it. Hopefully, you would get your money's worth out of it, but are you going to be happy with your purchase? Probably not, because as we mentioned before, no piece of tech stays the latest for long, and no fashion remains on trend for long either. You're always going to own something which is outdated or left behind, pushing you to replace it sooner than you should. As a result of this, you're wasting money. You might as well throw it into the air and watch the breeze carry it away!

On the other hand, investing your cash into experiences is a far more worthwhile endeavour. For instance, the money you save from not buying material items could be put to one side for a few months and then you may have enough to go away somewhere nice on vacation. The time you spend in whatever location you choose will bring you memories which will always remain with you, and you'll get to see a new place, perhaps learn a few words of a new language, experience a new culture, try new foods. Can you see how these things are so much more worthwhile and valuable than buying a new pair of shoes, or a new phone?

It doesn't have to be travel, it can be any other type of experience too. For instance, you will be able to afford to treat your parents to dinner out somewhere nice, or maybe a day out with your kids or partner. This is something they will appreciate, and it means you get to spend quality time together, making memories and taking many photographs. These are important things in life – quality time and good memories.

You could also invest that cash into something which will benefit you in the long-term- learning. How about starting a new course, perhaps at the local college or maybe starting an online course with a distance learning organisation? This will benefit you by learning new knowledge, skills, giving you confidence, and also perhaps boosting your career options in the future.

All of this is extremely possible, simply by not spending cash on material items. The experience you have will never leave you, it will never break, it will never go out of fashion, and it will never be thrown away. In the future, when you are much older, you will look back on those experiences and smile, remembering them for the wonderful times they were. You probably won't look back when you're older and think about the time you purchase a new iPhone.

Can you see the difference? Investing in experiences is always far more worthwhile than investing in material possessions.

Strategies For Reusing, Recycling, and Donating Existing Possessions

When you initially begin your new minimalist lifestyle, you will need to declutter, and that is something we're going to cover in far more detail in our next chapter. Decluttering is not as simple as throwing things out and thinking you've achieved minimalism because you need to do something useful with the items you no longer need.

Minimalism does not teach you to throw things away needlessly. Yes, you are decluttering, but you need to do something with the things you no longer need, something which will benefit you and someone else if at all possible. There are a few ways you can do this - you can reuse an item, you can recycle an item, or you can donate an item.

All these methods are distinctly different.

If you choose to reuse an item, this means you can change the way it looks or the purpose for which you use it. For instance, maybe you have an old sofa that is ripped or broken but you still like it. You don't have to throw it out and buy a new one, because you can fix the problem, and cover it over to make it look completely new. You can change the entire decor of the sofa and make it look completely different, but you're not bending to consumerism and buying a new sofa for a hugely inflated price. This is what we mean when we say 'reuse'.

On the other hand, you could recycle your stuff. When you recycle something, you could argue that it overlaps with reusing because you're recycling what you are using it for and avoiding throw it out. This is true, but recycling, in this case, means giving it to a specific recycling unit and letting them turn it into something else entirely. For example, we recycle our plastic bottles so that they can be regenerated and therefore save the environment. You're doing a wonderful thing for the planet and you're getting rid of the items that you no longer, need, ticking the decluttering box.

Finally, you could donate items and allow someone else to use them. Just because you no longer need something or want something doesn't mean that another person won't be able to find a very good use for it. Not everyone is as lucky or as affluent especially in some parts of third world countries like India or Africa. This means that they aren't able to purchase new items, but they still need them. For instance, a young, newly married couple might be expecting a child and moving into a new home. They need many things for their new house, but they don't have the cash to purchase them because of the new baby. In this case, any household furniture items you can gift them will go to such a great cause. Can you imagine the good deed you're doing and how great you'll feel as a result? You're actually making a difference to someone's life, simply by de-cluttering your home and being careful with what you choose to do with the items you no longer need.

The same goes for any clothes that you decide you're not going to wear, don't fit you, or you simply don't want. You don't have to throw them out, and you don't have to go around listing everything on eBay either - how about donating them to a charity shop and allowing someone to purchase them, with benefit to the charity of your choice? You can choose a charity shop which has a special place in your heart, e.g. cancer research, animal welfare, or helping the elderly, to name just a few. It's completely up to you which charity you go for, but anything you donate will be very gratefully received and will make a huge difference to someone else.

As you can see, part of living the minimalist lifestyle isn't just about decluttering and being clearer in your own mind, it's also about perhaps helping others along the way. Consider it good Karma!

It's completely up to you which option you go for, and whether you want to reuse something or gift it to a worthwhile cause. What you should do is ask yourself which option is best before you make a decision. The point is that you're not throwing away for no reason and you're not buying for equally no reason.

How to Avoid Compulsive Spending, Particularly Online

One of the biggest problems with today's society is that spending cash is oh-so-easy. Nowadays, we don't have to wait for the shops to open and for good weather so we can head out and browse the goods on offer, we can do it from the comfort of our own home; we don't even have to get dressed! Online shopping is a wonderful invention, but it is also a double-edged sword.

Temptation can be very high and that means you could end up spending cash without even meaning to. For instance, in the past have you purchased goods because you were bored? Boredom spending is one of the biggest culprits when it comes to overspending and general materialism. In addition, have you found that when you're feeling down or emotional, a quick online shopping hit makes you feel better? Emotional shopping is another reason for overspending.

Compulsive spending doesn't have to be an online thing, because both boredom and emotional shopping habits are usually formed on the High Street first and foremost. It's really about learning to recognise your habits and deal with them in better ways. For instance, if you shop because you're bored, try and busy your mind with more productive things, such as going to the gym, learning something new, or going for a walk. These will all serve you far better than purchasing something new and will save you a lot of cash in the process.

So, how can you avoid those compulsive spending sprees, either online or at the High Street? Here are a few tips.

- Before you head off on a shopping spree, either in person or virtually, ask yourself why. Identify what is pushing you to want to shop - are you hungry, thirsty, bored, tired, emotional, upset? Why do you want to shop?

- Push the thought from your mind and instead busy your mind with something more constructive. For instance, go for a walk, do some exercise, make a meal. Do something which takes your mind off the idea of shopping, and you're likely to find that it disappears.

- If online shopping is your tipple, how about having a fake hit? This might get you through the first few weeks of learning to wean yourself off materialism. Look at the items all you want, and even place them in your basket, but then click off the page and don't purchase anything. Walk away and wait, overnight if possible. By the time you go back to it, you'll no longer want the items and most of them will have sold out!

- Move your money out of any account which can be used to shop online. If you don't have the cash in the right place, you can't buy anything, and again, the need to purchase will disappear.

- Give yourself one treat every month. This shouldn't be something large, it should be something small but something you will look forward to. This will tackle the need to compulsively spend cash, and whatever you do buy, you'll value and enjoy far more as a result. Over time, wean yourself off this habit, and you'll be firmly into the minimalistic mindset.

These are all good ways to tackle compulsive spending, but the most important thing is to ask yourself why you want to spend. If you actually need the product, fine, go ahead and buy it; if you don't need it, you should examine what is pushing you. If you tend to shop when you're feeling emotional, how about having a chat with a friend and getting everything out? That way you'll tackle the problem, feel better, and you won't have spent any cash at all. If you feel like shopping because you're bored, do something more interesting which takes your mind off it.

Being mindful is the best way to tackle compulsive spending, and the more you question your motives, the more you will begin to recognise that they aren't good enough reasons for ruining your new minimalist endeavours or ruin your bank account.

Defining Your Budget - Reviewing Your Financial Position & Setting Long and Short Term Goals

Now we need to talk about budgeting. Whilst this isn't the most glamorous subject in the world, it is one which is necessary for a life which gives you enough. For instance, if you don't budget, how can you be sure that you're going to have enough money to make it until the end of the month? How can you be sure that your bills are going to be paid? You can't!

We mentioned earlier about how budgeting and minimalism work together very closely. Both are designed to give you enough to live with, and whilst minimalism is more about having a specific mindset and learning to do more with less, budgeting can teach you the same thing. A cleverly designed budget can actually give you more cash over the long-term, because you're examining the things that you're spending money on, and you're making changes where necessary. Effective budgeting can also allow you to make financial goals and save up for experiences which you'll remember for a lifetime. In order to set yourself a budget, follow these easy steps:

- Write down the amount of cash you have coming into your household every month

- In a separate space, write down the outgoings you need to pay every month, e.g. rent, bills, fuel costs, debts, telephone costs, etc

- Add up the total number of outgoings to give you two figures - your incomings and your outgoings

- Subtract the outgoings from your incomings to give you a surplus figure

- This figure is what you have spare every month, and is classed as your disposable income

If you have a good amount as disposable income, you're doing well in your budgeting endeavours. If on the other hand, you've noticed that your outgoings are equal to or more than the money you have coming in, you need to make drastic changes.

Look at the list of things you have going out of your household every month. Is there anything which you can get rid of? For instance, do you need to have such a high cellphone package every month? Can you live with less data and make use of your wifi instead? This will save you cash. Do you have any monthly payments which you no longer make use of, e.g. a gym membership or insurance packages which you don't need? These are all areas to look at, especially insurance. In some cases, you are doubled up on protection, and you could cancel one policy and save yourself cash on monthly payments.

By streamlining your outgoings, you're effectively cluttering your finances and this is all part of living a minimalistic lifestyle. The perk is that doing this gives you more money!

Now you need to decide what you're going to do with your surplus cash, e.g. your disposable income. This is where you need to think carefully and you need to make short term and long term goals as a result. What you decide to aim for will give you those experiences we talked about earlier. For instance, do you want to go away on vacation? Do you want to save cash to go back to school and learn something new? Do you want to have the cash to take your parents away somewhere wonderful? These are experiences which come into the 'money can't buy' category, but the reality is that if you want these things, you need to save for them.

With this in mind, from your disposable income identify an amount you can save per month. How much you want to save depends on what your short term and long term goals are.

A short term goal is defined as something you want to achieve perhaps within the next year, so a vacation with family could fall into this category. A long term goal is something which could take five years plus to achieve. If you want to save for the deposit on a new home, this is a long term goal.

Identifying how much to save every month should allow you to reach both your short and long term goals, but you also need to decide where to save that cash. If you keep it in your bank account, you're going to dib into it without realising and as a result, you'll actually lose money rather than save it. This is why you should consider transferring your savings every month into a high-interest savings account. You should avoid having a cash card for this account, so you have to go to a lot of effort to draw out the cash - this means you're less likely to touch it!

A minimalistic lifestyle gives you more cash, simply because you're far more wary of what you spend money on and you're less inclined towards mass consumerism. Not being concerned with buying the latest fashions or the latest tech will actually line your bank account far more than you could ever have imagined, and budgeting is something which will help you achieve your aims.

Make sure that you are completely honest and realistic when designing a budget, and that you don't miss out any items which you need to pay every month, simply because you don't want to face up to them. If you have debts, do what you can to pay them off. By doing this, you'll feel happier, freer, and it will all contribute toward the contentment which minimalism will give you overall. Start with the smaller debts and pay them off. Once you've done that, tackle the larger ones, or the ones with a higher interest rate. It might take some time, but in the future, when you'll be debt-free and you'll be pleased that you put in the effort.

What We Have Learnt in This Chapter

In this chapter, we have talked about cash and what to do with items that you no longer need. We've covered a lot of information, so take your time digesting it and read over anything you're not sure of.

One of the key takeaways from this chapter was learning what to do with any items that you decide you no longer need. Do not simply throw these items away. That is a huge waste! Part of the minimalist lifestyle is about gifting items and reusing, recycling and helping those who might need it. So, redesign and reuse items if you can, choose to recycle items if you want to, and gift or donate items if you choose to do that. Make sure you choose a person or a cause which is close to your heart and you'll feel great about it afterwards.

We talked about the fact that experiences are far more worthwhile and rewarding than any material good. Whilst it's wrong to say you can't put a price on a vacation to somewhere amazing, you do have to look at the fact that it is an experience and not a product to own. You will meet people, experience cultures and have memories which will blow your mind, and which you will remember forever. A new phone or a new product won't do that for you.

We also talked about how to avoid compulsive spending, especially online. So many of us get an urge to spend cash simply because we're bored, or because we can. Putting into place mechanisms to ensure this doesn't happen means that you will be less likely to make those impulse purchases, and you'll save cash as a result!

Finally, we talked in detail about budgeting and what you can do to give yourself more cash from your monthly income. This extra cash can, therefore, be saved to help you reach your short and long term goals. Again, this is far more rewarding than any new laptop, new game, new phone, or a new piece of fashion.

Chapter 6: Decluttering Your Home

We cannot talk about the minimalist lifestyle and not cover how to actually declutter your home. Whilst decluttering your mind, changing your entire mindset, and arranging a more favourable financial situation is all part and parcel of minimalism, the starting point and perhaps the most famous part, is about decluttering your living space.

So, how do you actually start?

The single best way to approach this rather large task is to work in small milestones. Don't get up one day and decide that you're going to declutter and that's the job done. It will certainly take you more than one day to declutter your living space, and it will probably take you several weeks to complete the process! This is something you need to make peace with before you start.

You should also be aware of the fact that it might be harder than you think, e.g. you will need to think twice or even three times before you decide what to throw out, what to reuse, what to recycle, and what to donate.

For that reason, work on one section at a time. Let's go through a few milestones you should begin with, working on one at a time.

Wardrobes

It's a good idea to start with wardrobe for the single reason that this is one of the biggest hoarding spots for most people! The amount of things you will find in the average wardrobe is staggering and the majority are never worn or used. It's not even just clothes you'll find, as there will be shoes and all manner of other accessories and items that probably don't even traditionally belong in this space!

Clearing out your wardrobe will instantly give you a sense of calm and along with the garage or shed, will probably end up being the space which you remove most clutter from. Dedicate a whole day to your wardrobe, and by that, we mean one day per wardrobe! Don't rush this process, as it needs to be a careful and intentional act. Remember, minimalism is an intention to live with less than you have, and simply all you need. If you throw things out randomly or you keep things that you don't really need, you're not actually adhering to the mindset of minimalism at all.

Start with one wardrobe and open both doors and all the drawers, if there are any. If there is anything stored on top of the wardrobe, bring that down also. Work in sections, to avoid overwhelming yourself. For instance, if you have clutter on top of your wardrobe, work with that first, before you move onto the drawers. Once you've done those sections, move to the bottom section of the wardrobe (a key place where most people hoard things), and then work on the hanging section.

A few key points to remember here:

- If you have not worn something for the last six months, put it on the declutter pile

- Equally, if something does not fit you, it should go on that pile and not be kept 'just in case' it fits again in the future

- If you don't feel comfortable in a piece of clothing, that should also go on the declutter pile. You need to keep the clothes that you wear and which you like, not clothes which are there from years ago

- Shoes which are very uncomfortable or for extremely special occasions should go on the declutter pile. Basically, if you haven't worn them in the last six months, they should go

- Shoes which are damaged or old in some way, e.g. they have a slight split on the sole, should be decluttered

- Look at the bags and purses you own and streamline it down to one per every occasion, e.g. one beach bag, one everyday bag, one evening out bag, one work bag/laptop bag. The others should be decluttered

- The same rules apply for accessories. Don't keep things like hats, scarves, gloves, decorative pieces just because you might wear them one day. If they haven't seen the light of day for six months, they should be decluttered also

Do you have shoe boxes in your wardrobe which are full of random pieces of junk or memorable pieces? Many people do. If this is the case, cast these to one side and work through them more methodically. Special memory pieces need to have a little extra thought attached to them, but in this case, you could think about gifting these items to a loved one for them to keep, rather than you having them and cluttering up your wardrobe.

At the end of your wardrobe cleanse, you should have only clothes, shoes, bag, and accessories which you wear regularly, which suit you, and which are comfortable. You should not have anything on the top of your wardrobe and there should be nothing on the bottom section either. If you have drawers in your wardrobe, these should be streamlined and neatly organised in the same way. For instance, socks in one drawer, underwear in another, nightwear in a different drawer. Part of the decluttering process when working towards minimalism is also about organising your life for a clearer mind.

Now you need to ask yourself what you're going to do with your decluttered wardrobe items. This particular section is quite easy because it's not likely that you will choose to reuse or recycle clothes, shoes, bags, or accessories. What you will probably opt to do in this case is to donate the items you don't want. If any are broken, ripped, or in a poor state, you can throw those away, but the good condition items should be bagged up and either given to someone to wear, e.g. a friend or loved one, or taken to a charity shop of your choice.

If you have walk-in wardrobes or closets, you'll need to think about spending more time in these areas. Make sure that by the end of your wardrobe declutter, you have nothing but the things you really need. The clean and tidy state you leave your bedroom in will no doubt spur you on to continue your decluttering efforts.

Kitchen

Next up you need to head to the kitchen. This is an area which is going to take you some time. The reason for this is because most people have all manner of kitchen appliances lurking inside their cupboards which haven't seen the light of day for many years. We tend to buy every new gadget that comes along, thinking that it's going to come in very handy when we have people over for dinner, or when a birthday party takes place. The reality is that people don't come over for dinner so frequently, and when they do, you don't think to use that appliance! The same can be said for future birthday parties or phantom get-togethers!

Work through your kitchen in sections, to avoid making it a huge job which overwhelms you completely. It's also likely that throughout the time of you decluttering your kitchen, you're going to need to use it at some point, e.g. to make dinner. Don't rush your kitchen declutter, and it could be that it takes a day or two. Working on one section will mean that you can still use the space at the same time.

The easiest space to start with is your fridge. Throw out whatever is old. That's one very easy job. With the fridge decluttered, move onto your food cupboards. Discard of any food items which are past their sell-by date (admittedly everyone has several lurking in there), as well as any items of questionable quality. Again, most people have a few, such as flour that's been in there for a while, or baking powder which has never been used. Obviously, as you declutter you will mostly end up cleaning a bit at the same time.

The best way to look at all of this is to use visualisation. As you throw something away, picture negative energy being thrown away at the same time. As you clean up afterwards, picture bad luck and clutter being discarded. You'll bring in fresh energy as a result of taking this right action.

Once your fridge and food cupboards are decluttered, it's time to tackle the lower cupboards and drawers, which normally house the random kitchen appliances. For every piece of equipment, ask yourself whether you have used it in the last six months. Use the same thought process that you did with your wardrobe. If you have never turned that alliance on, or it's so lined with dust that you can't even tell what it is, that's a good sign that it should go on the declutter pile. Only keep the appliances that you use regularly, e.g. food processor, blender, toaster, kettle, etc.

You should also apply the same line of thinking to your cutlery and plates, etc. Do you have countless plates which you never use? For instance, are you a family of four but you have twelve plates? It's very unlikely that you ever have that many people over for dinner, so perhaps you should think about decluttering a few, perhaps gifting them to someone who is setting up a new home.

By the end of your kitchen decluttering, again, you should only have what you need and what you use on a regular basis. Everything else needs to be decluttered, but what do you do with it? If you have appliances that you do not use but which work perfectly well, you could gift them to someone who needs them, or you could recycle them. Many companies will take back old appliances in order to be recycled. These are then repackaged and sold second hand.

Remember, you do not need three sieves, you don't need four chopping boards, and you don't need eighteen mugs when there are only four of you. Ask yourself if you really need every single item, and declutter what you honestly don't need.

Bathrooms

The bathroom decluttering shouldn't be a particularly lengthy process, but if you have many toiletry items that you don't use, and you simply have them for decoration, it's time to get rid of those.

Give everything a really good clean as you declutter, and get rid of any decorative items that you have sitting around, e.g. rubber ducks or plaques. You don't need these things and they don't work well with the minimalist lifestyle. Remember, only keep what you need.

Any toiletries, e.g. fancy shower gels or bath lotions which have been there for years, simply because they look good, it's time to throw them out. The contents have probably long gone past their best, and they will quite frankly bring you out in a rash! Those need to be binned and decluttered with the rest of the items that you do not use.

It's unlikely that you will decide to recycle, reuse, or donate any items from your bathroom, so in this case, they'll mostly go into the trash pile. The reason for this is simply to enforce proper hygiene.

Living Room

The biggest bug-bear with a living room space is likely to be decorative items or ornaments which simply gather dust. We are not suggesting that you need to throw out photographs that hold significance for you because they can stay on your walls quite happily as part of the minimalist lifestyle. Instead, you need to think about ornaments that don't really mean anything. Again, these can be added to the declutter pile.

Do you have any pieces of furniture which are simply there for no reason? For instance, do you have two sofas when you only need one? Do you have two armchairs which are never sat in? Do you have decorative storage units which are really used to store clutter? Decluttering isn't just about small things, it's also about large pieces of furniture. In this case, you should also look at any pieces of furniture that you really don't want to throw out, because you do use them, but which have passed their best. Sofas which have rips can be repaired. Tables which are scratched can be repainted. Chairs which got faded and are out of fashion can be covered over with better fabric. All you need to do is check out YouTube and find out how to do it. Perhaps you'll find a new hobby you love!

Sofas and chairs are quite expensive to replace, so if you can reuse any old pieces you'll find costs saved instantly. Any decorative items that you do not use should go on the decluttering pile, in fact, any ornaments or unneeded items should certainly be decluttered. Your living room should be a place of comfort and serenity and having far too many plants, ornaments, pictures, cushions and random carpets everywhere simply doesn't sit in line with the minimalist scene! Whilst we're not suggesting your living space should be bare, it should be functional and comfortable only.

Any items you choose to declutter from your living room, you need to think carefully about what to do with them, as these have value. Think about whether you can reuse any items as we described above, and think about whether you want to recycle or donate. There are many people who are lacking in household furniture items, who can't afford to buy them for themselves. By gifting any items you no longer use, you're doing a great deed.

Bedrooms

This is a spot which is going to take you a good amount of time! If you have children, decluttering their bedrooms will be a tough business, and we're going to talk in a later chapter about how to help your family adapt to the minimalist lifestyle as well. For now, let's talk about adult bedrooms because we will cover later how to declutter a child's bedroom.

You've already tackled the wardrobes, so it's likely that the rest of the process will be quicker. If you have cupboards or shelves in your bedroom, make sure you pull everything out and examine each item in terms of long term usage. Make sure those decorative items are removed, just as they were in the living room. Minimalism means exactly that - minimal items, only the ones you need! Most of us are guilty of too much decorative clutter in our bedrooms, so this is something which you need to focus your time on.

Once you finalize the items that you donot need, you should then decide on what to do with them. Again, ask yourself the same question - can you reuse it, or can it be donated? Many people will purchase such items from a charity shop, so you could be helping a good cause by donating the bedroom items you don't need.

Garage/Sheds

Probably one of the spaces in your home which is going to take the longest to declutter is your sheds and garage space if you have one. If you don't have a garage or a shed, you probably have a loft or another storage area which needs to be focused on. Regardless of which space you have, you should adopt the same thought process.

Work in small areas and be particularly ruthless. We tend to place all of our junk into these spaces because it is out of the way, but most of the time we do not use or want what is in there. It is often a case of the scenario known as 'out of sight, out of mind'. And also, getting rid of large items, such as lawn mowers or car parts that aren't needed, is such a big job. Decluttering these items will free up so much space, but will also clear your mind. The items in this space can often be gifted, reused, or recycled very easily. They make particularly good choices when you decide to put up a yard sale.

There may be items you do need, such as your lawnmower, car maintenance items, and the likes, but the high likelihood is that whatever is in that space is not used regularly. Boxes that you store in the garage with things from times gone by aren't needed. Yes, they are sentimental but are your memories in your mind or in your garage? Photos are something different because these are something you can keep, but mixtapes from your first love, clothes that your child wore when they were a baby, and keys given to you on your 18th birthday, this, believe it or not, is clutter.

You have a few options when it comes to what to do with these items and it depends on what they are. Large machinery items may be able to get recycled. It's often the case that even if they don't work, there are many people out there who can work their magic and regenerate them for someone else to use at a later date. You could also donate these to a person who needs it, or a charity shop once more. Most mechanical items can be recycled and this is probably the safest bet with this category of items.

By the end of clearing out your garage or shed, you should have a huge amount of extra space. This does not mean you have extra space in which to store more clutter, but a space which remains that way, and gives you extra room to move around freely and operate effectively.

What We Have Learnt in This Chapter

We've talked about the main areas of the house which need to be decluttered and giving you a lot of advice on how to do it. It will take time, so don't rush it. Decluttering an entire house can take weeks in some cases, and it's even possible that you won't do it right in the first place. If you choose to keep things, go back over it in a week or so and ask yourself again whether you really need it. The chances are that by the time you have immersed yourself in the minimalist lifestyle a little more, you'll think differently about any items that you choose to keep in your home. For that reason, go back over your decluttered spaces once more, perhaps in a month or two.

We've also talked about the specific items that you might be able to reuse, recycle or donate to someone or a charity shop of your choice. You'll probably have several bags of items by the end of your decluttering efforts, so perhaps redirect your items where they need to go after every room, so you don't end up with too much to transport at one time. Whilst charity shops are very grateful for anything you donate, you should check if it's a good option to overload them with new stock all at once.

With every single room that you declutter, you will notice your mind clearing and your spirits lifting. The more you do, the greater the benefits you will feel and you'll also be energised to continue onwards. Decluttering can actually be very addictive once you get it going. So Happy Clearing!

Chapter 7: Freeing up Your Mental Space

In the previous chapter, we talked about how to declutter your physical space, i.e. your home, but now we need to talk about how to declutter your mental space. This is just as important as the actual space around you i.e., the things you can touch. By freeing up space in your mind you are giving yourself the chance to be calm, be content, and not to be overwhelmed or stressed with everything going on around you.

With the busy and stressful lives we lead these days, it can be very easy to be running from one task to another, and never really getting anything finished. Trying to multi-task simply leads to being overloaded with too much work, and then trying to remember a million things at once? It's a recipe for pressure!

Once you declutter your physical space, you'll probably already feel a lot calmer and decluttered in your mind, but the hard work doesn't end there. You now need to spend some time with your energy and attention turned inwards. Don't be tempted to jump over this step, simply because you think it isn't as important as the physical decluttering; in some ways, it is more important because the power of your mind is so great.

In this chapter, we're going to talk about the things you need to ditch, i.e. the things that should hold no space or attention in your brain. We're also going to talk about a few darker issues which many people deal with, e.g.

overcoming traumas that have happened in the past, and a need to fill an empty space. These are all key issues which we need to face, talk about, and overcome, in order to be able to fully embrace and enjoy the minimalist lifestyle and mindset.

Decluttering Your Mind

Our heads are full of useless information, memories we don't really need, and opinions from other people. Most of the things we hold in our heads are completely unnecessary and tend to occupy the space we should be using for the important things like enriching memories, positive beliefs, and our own sense of confidence and self-esteem.

It's time to sit down and have a mind decluttering session, just as you did with your home. You'll need to dedicate a good amount of time to this, and don't expect it to show results or take effect immediately. Whenever you try and change mindsets or alter any thinking pattern, it's very easy to expect results straight away, and then become disheartened when they don't appear. Any type of mindset training is about a snowball effect, so be patient and have faith that the results will show!

Try this exercise:

- Grab a pen and paper, and sit yourself down somewhere quiet, where you're not going to be bothered, making yourself comfortable. Make sure your phone is on silent or turned off, you don't need to be disturbed at this point. It's also a good idea to make the time for this exercise when you don't have to rush off to do anything, so your mind is clear and not on something else

- Write down what you are thinking right now. In fact, whenever a thought pops into your head, write it down

- Then turn your attention to the things you think about most. For instance, is there a worry or thought which you spend a lot of time considering? Write it down

- On a daily basis, what are the thoughts and memories which consume the majority of your time? Again, write them down. What you're trying to do here is get an idea, a very clear idea and inventory, of what you spend most of your time thinking about. This will help you decide what is useful and what isn't

- Next, ask yourself if you consider yourself to be stressed. If the answer is yes, what are you stressed about? Write it down

- Do you have any recurring dreams or nightmares? Write them down in as much detail as you can

By the end of this exercise, you will probably have a very long list of things which occupy your mind during your waking hours, as well as any recurring dreams which are interfering with your sleep.

Now grab a different coloured pen. You're going to put a different coloured line through every thought or issue you have written down which is negative, unhelpful, unnecessary, or simply pointless. You will probably realise that you have marked off the overwhelming majority of points! Every time you put a line through an item, visualise it being cast away. Say the words if you need to. Like 'goodbye' or 'let it go' or words to that effect, basically something which resonates in your mind and confirms that this point is not necessary for your mind.

Some people find it useful to burn the piece of paper and continue to visualise those thoughts being destroyed. This might be a useful tool for you also. Don't worry about destroying the useful or good points you wrote down, these will remain because you have confirmed they need to stay, by not crossing them off.

Repeat this exercise weekly, and you should notice that as you get more into the minimalist lifestyle, your list of pointless or cluttered thoughts gets smaller and smaller. Also make sure to spend more time on yourself, e.g. exercising, going outside and having a walk rather than staying in, heading into nature, spending time with loved ones and friends. A little self-care can do wonders for distracting the brain from thoughts that really aren't useful. The lesser time you spend dedicated to thinking about them, the weaker they become, and therefore the less space they will take up. In the end, they will disappear into thin air and you'll be left with more & clearer headspace to work with.

Part of decluttering your mind is also about looking at the friendships and relationships you have in your life. Do you have toxic connections? If so, those connections need to be terminated. If someone brings nothing positive to your life, if they spend most of the time dragging you down, making you feel less than adequate, or always bringing drama, perhaps ask yourself whether you need this added stress? The answer will always be 'no', and in that case, you should add them to the declutter pile too, as harsh as it may sound. But a word of caution: it is better to take your time and do it gently with some relationships. Let time do the breaking as you slowly detach yourself from your harmful relationships.

Reducing Unnecessary Limiting Beliefs

Most of us have some kind of belief system in our lives. This doesn't necessarily have to be religious, and it can be something else, e.g. cultural, something we have learnt since childhood, or an opinion which we have, but we're probably not quite sure where it came from. The problem is, a belief is all very well and good when it enriches your life and encourages you to achieve success and be happy, but when it limits you in some way, it's a negative thing, and not at all positive.

For instance, most of us have a society-placed belief in our minds that we should be married and have children by the age of 35, otherwise we're too old. That is rubbish. What if you don't want to get married? What if you don't want children? What if you do but you want to wait until you're 40? None of it matters as far as your truth and experience of life are concerned.

It's important to think about the beliefs you have and to decide whether they are limiting and negative, or empowering and positive. Again, take some time sitting and writing down the things which you believe in your life, the things which might have held you back in the past. Once you write something down, really question it. Why do you believe it? Why is it so important? Does it limit you at all? If it does limit you and it doesn't encourage you, it's time to overcome that belief and to replace it with something which is altogether more positive.

Challenge whatever you think and really ask yourself what is important in life. It isn't important to be so-called 'settled down' by any age, the important thing is that you're happy, regardless of your age. That is just one example, and there are far more. What if you're studying for a particular degree at university, perhaps to become a certain type of professional, e.g. a doctor, but you really don't feel like you're enjoying it? You believe you have to complete your studies because your family would be disappointed otherwise, but you would much rather do something creative with your life. Should you continue because you believe you have to? Or, should you face the problem, sort it out and follow the path that makes you happy? The choice you make will depend on how empowering your beliefs are. So you need to pay close attention to them with regular tweaking if necessary.

Beliefs are great when they encourage and nurture, but they are extremely damaging when they limit. Take some time now to clear your mind of the ones which limit you in any way.

Overcoming Past Trauma

You might wonder what facing up to past traumas has to do with living a minimalist life, but it's about clearing your life of negative energies. If a past traumatic event is still holding you hostage in your mind, it needs to be decluttered along with everything else. Of course, this is not an easy task, and it may be one which requires painful introspection and possible help to overcome the painful memories which are unearthed.

Whatever the trauma is, be it a very serious event or something which you simply deem to have affected you in a traumatic way, it's important to face it head on in the best way you can. If the problem is serious, and if it does unearth very painful memories for you, the single best route here is to contact a health care professional and access counselling services. Without a doubt, overcoming such problems will free you from their grips, and will leave you much lighter and more able to reach happiness in the future. The negativity that sits within you from past traumas can be overcome, but often a bit difficult and frustrating to do so. But it's important to not give up, however – have faith in your own strength and seek appropriate guidance when you can.

Talk it out, cry it out, do whatever you need to do in the healthiest of ways to overcome the trauma and cast it away. In so many cases, professional help, such as therapy, is a fantastic option.

Overcoming the Need to Fill the Emptiness

One reason why people tend to buy products they don't need, become addicted to shopping, or simply indulge in impulsive purchases, is because they have an unfilled void within them. Perhaps they have lost someone they love and aren't dealing with the grief so well, or perhaps they are dealing with heartbreak and the failure of a relationship. These are just two examples, but there are many more reasons why someone may feel a sense of emptiness inside.

The thing is, buying something is not going to make you feel whole. It might make you feel light on your feet for a few hours, but it will fade away and the lightness will be replaced by a heaviness, and probably a sense of guilt for the money you spent.

Instead of heading to the shops or your laptop when you feel down or unfulfilled, explore the reason why instead. What is it that is making you feel this way? What are you lacking in your life? Are you actually lacking anything, or it is more that you are striving for something and you haven't achieved it yet? True happiness really does come from within, and it doesn't come from a credit card purchase or dipping into your savings. If you are lacking something, identify what it is and then put a plan into action to help you get it. Even better, ask yourself why you're craving it so badly and why it is affecting your life to such a degree.

Most of the time, a void of emptiness comes down to confidence. You can overcome such issues, but it really is all in your mind. You need to focus, you need to be strong, and you need to build up your confidence to the point where you really believe that anything is possible - because it is. Once you get to this stage, you'll understand that the only person who can fill any void within you is you. You can't rely on someone or something else to make you feel whole, and shopping or owning the latest products on the market is not going to do it either.

The power is within you, you just have to know how to tap into it. Introspection and understanding why minimalism can help you achieve this sense of calm is vital. Essentially, minimalism will bring you face to face with this internal void and the more time you spend dealing with it, the better you get.

What We Have Learnt in This Chapter

In this chapter, we've delved quite deeply into the inner psyche and we've asked a lot of difficult questions. Decluttering your mind is not as simple as saying 'be gone bad thoughts' and then expecting it to work. Decluttering takes time, it takes effort, and it also takes strength. You need to understand why you are thinking the way you are, and what you are lacking. By doing that, you'll be able to overcome any problems or limitations which have been holding you back in the past, and you'll be free to fly.

It's true that when you cast away baggage from the past, you have a light feeling. This is contentment. This is a true sense of happiness and confidence. That is what you are aiming for. When you declutter your mind and achieve a minimalist mindset and lifestyle, you can look forward to that feeling probably almost every day of your life! We're not suggesting that with this lifestyle you're never going to feel down again, or you're never going to have a bad day because that's part of human life, but you will have the power and confidence to overcome those issues, much more effectively and easily than you would otherwise.

If physical decluttering takes time, mental decluttering takes a lot longer. Bear with it and persevere. The end results are more than worth it!

Chapter 8: Minimalism For Family Life

Is it possible to live a minimalistic family life? The answer is undoubtedly yes.

A family which does minimalism together will be a very happy, positive, and confident family. By raising children who understand the real value of owning items, rather than always wanting something new, you're raising well-rounded, positive, and respectful children. How many times have you seen a child having a tantrum in a supermarket because their mother or father refused to buy them something from the toy aisle? They were told 'no' and because they did not like the answer, they decided to scream and shout instead.

This is partly child-like nature, but it is also about the child not understanding the value of money. For instance, if that child is a little older, perhaps older than 10, they should understand that any item on that toy aisle costs money, and that money has to be earned. Screaming and shouting should not end in getting what they want!

This is part and parcel of why a minimalistic family is not about children going without and is actually about enriching a child's life to the point where they gain something truly beneficial - respect and understanding of value.

Of course, this doesn't mean that a child within a minimalist family should never own toys and never have new things, because of course children will be children, and toys are part and parcel of their education and development. What minimalism says about this however is that moderation is key. Children should have the things they need, not the things they necessarily always want, and if they want something else, they should work for it in the future and then buy it for themselves. This will teach them the value of hard work, perseverance and discipline. In the future, it will be their choice whether they live a minimalistic life or not.

This section is somewhat contentious because many people will go through it and think that it's a bit harsh or unkind to children. It's not. I'm in no way suggesting that a child should go without, but in this day and age, so many children are spoiled, whilst so many other children are going without even the most basic of human needs, e.g. food due to famine. Teaching a child about the value of money, and also teaching them that they are lucky to have the things they have, will allow them to grow up to be well-mannered and appreciative, and not simply expecting things to be handed to them on a silver platter.

How the Minimalistic Life Can Enrich Relationships With Loved Ones

One of the major benefits of the minimalist life is that it can help to really boost the relationships you have with those around you. You're not so focused on owning the latest gadget or fashion item, and you're not so constantly tied to your phone that you never look up to find out if someone is smiling or frowning. Minimalism teaches you to slow down, be mindful, and appreciate the things around you, relationships with family and friends included.

Remember, by following a minimalist lifestyle you will have more money. That's a simple, common sense fact; if you're not spending cash, you have it spare. That money can be put towards experiences, as we mentioned before. Those experiences can be shared with family and friends and can include vacations, evenings out, and simply being together away from the house. Sharing these experiences binds you together for life, because you share memories of those amazing times, which you'll talk about when you're older. If you have children in the future, you'll tell them about those times, and the memories will be passed on.

Far too many families and friends are estranged or disconnected because of the modern day obsession with owning material goods or being constantly attached to a phone. Being more aware of those around you is the fast-track towards better relationships. Talk instead of keeping quiet, spend time instead of sending a text, and do things together rather than just saying 'one day'. All of these things will enrich your relationships and make your life much more fulfilling and valuable as a result.

How to Declutter When You Have Children

There is one sticking point of living the minimalist family life, and that is decluttering the home when you have children. We mentioned this in passing earlier on, and we will cover it in more detail now.

You've cleaned out the entire home and you have bagfuls of things to donate, recycle, or reuse. Great news. There is one room left untouched, however - the kids' room.

Children's bedrooms often look like a cacophony of colour and mess and usually have countless toys and other items within them. Should you be ruthless with the contents of that room like you have been with all the others? Not quite so ruthless is the best answer.

The following rules really sum it up perfectly:

- Declutter your child's home when they are at school, nursery, or out on a play date
- Throw away any toys that do not work anymore, or have broken pieces
- Make sure every toy you decide to keep has somewhere to live
- If your child has barely had the toy out of the box, gift it to another child who will play with it

- Do not keep toys simply because they were your child's first – if they aren't going to play with them now

By following these rules, your child will be left with the toys which work well, the toys they play with regularly, and it will be very easy to tidy up the room because all toys have a specific dedicated area. As you can see, it's the same principle as decluttering the rest of the house, and you're still keeping the things which your child loves - that's the whole point of minimalism after all; it's not about throwing everything unnecessary out and having only that which matter, it's about keeping the things you really need and being happy with it in so many ways.

Of course, there might be a few questions coming your way, like 'where is my jungle animals play set?'. You could get imaginative here and say that Santa took it away because a child with no toys needed it, or the tooth fairy, and that might suffice. The more likely scenario is that they will never ask where a certain toy has gone because they never played with it anyway!

You're also doing a great deed here because unused or unwanted toys can be gifted to children who don't have as much in their lives, via straightforward gifting or via a charity shop. You can also often box up unwanted toys these days and send them to children overseas, e.g. children in the third world or in war zones. The same goes for children's clothes, shoes, and blankets that are no longer used. That's such a wonderful thing to do with your unwanted items.

What We Have Learnt in This Chapter

In this chapter, we've talked about how minimalism can bring you far closer to your loved ones because you're not so focused on buying new things and general ownership. You have more time, you are more open-minded, and you have the cash to spend on experiences together, to create memories. Those are the things which are most important in life. We've also talked about the challenges of adopting a minimalistic lifestyle when you have children.

Most children living in western societies these days are extremely lucky, and most don't even realise it. Minimalism is a great way to teach children the value of money and about how lucky they are compared to other children in other parts of the world. This can be a very valuable lesson for a child to learn. Of course, minimalism doesn't mean throwing away all your child's toys and expecting them to understand! In order to declutter a child's bedroom, you should focus on the things they don't use or the things that are broken. From there, you can gift the items that they don't use, and you have a clearer space as a result. Your child will probably not even notice that most toys they never used have disappeared anyway!

A minimalistic family is generally a very happy, together, and content family.

Chapter 9: Adjusting to the Minimalist Lifestyle

Our final chapter is going to be about how we can adjust to the minimalist lifestyle. We have talked a little before about the fact that a minimalist lifestyle is not something which you can get by clicking your fingers and then adjust to it overnight. The deep-seated desire to purchase items and getting a kick out of it is something which will most likely take a while to overcome, just to be honest. Despite that, it can be done and perseverance will get you there. The journey is more than worth it, thanks to the benefits which will come your way.

First of all, however, we need to dedicate a whole chapter to the issues and challenges that might come your way at the start. By being aware of all of this, you are far better prepared to deal with it and therefore overcome it quickly. Nothing will be a surprise if you arm yourself with the necessary information beforehand. So, let's dive into the final piece of the jigsaw, helping you to move towards the minimalist lifestyle.

Initial Issues You Will Face

The first issue that will come your way is temptation. Consider this as the devil and angel on your shoulders. One is telling you that you need that item, the other is telling you that you don't. The angel is going to lead you in the right direction, whereas the devil is trying to derail your efforts. All you have to do is enable enough head space so that the angel's voice can get louder. This is where the mental decluttering exericses we talked about in chapter 7 will help massively.

You are going to need willpower in the beginning, and there might be times when you have a tough internal dialogue with yourself. Remember the benefits that a minimalist lifestyle will bring you, and always remember why you are doing it in the first place. If you can bring that to the front of your mind, you will overcome these times and you will come out of it stronger. The more you practice this willpower muscle, the stronger it will become, and the less you will have to exert for the same kind of response. In general, you will realize that it gets easier with time, and that this is simply a transitional period.

In many ways, you can compare it to smoking addiction. You are actually giving up something which has formed a habit. Your need to own and purchase items, i.e. materialism, is a mindset which has become deep-seated, and you need to use willpower to overcome it and to change your life in a different direction. Countless people stop smoking every single day successfully, so you can certainly overcome your need to own material items too.

Another issue is something you might find a little odd. The fact that you're not purchasing new things for the sake of it will mean that you have extra cash, and that's a great thing. What you might then be tempted to do is spend it! This is most likely to happen in the first month or so after you start your minimalist lifestyle, especially if you're not used to having spare cash at the end of every month. As a result, the 'red mist' comes down and you want to go shopping and spend that money. Have a plan, just like we mentioned with the budgeting section previously. This will help you overcome these moments of 'I have excess money', and save it towards something worthwhile instead.

A good idea is to have a visual reminder. For instance, if you're saving up to go on a family safari break in Kenya because it's something which has always been a dream, cut out a photo of a safari, with elephants, lions, the beautiful scenery etc, and stick it somewhere prominent. Whenever you feel the need to splurge, look at that photo as a reminder and you'll feel less inclined to let your good efforts go to waste.

The final challenge is likely to come from those around you who don't understand your new way of life. Not everyone is meant for the minimalist lifestyle, but we must all choose our own paths and allow others to do the same. If you are finding questions coming your way from people close to you who simply don't understand why you're embracing this new way of life, explain your reasons and leave it at that. You don't need to try and convince anyone that you're right or wrong, you simply need to do whatever makes you feel happy and at ease.

How to Meet Other Members of The Minimalist Community

Minimalism isn't just a thing that a few people practice, it's actually a worldwide community of people, and if you want to link up with other like-minded individuals, you can do just that. Check out social media boards, e.g. Facebook, and get chatting with other people who live the minimalist lifestyle. These people will be able to give you hints and tips to get you established, and can also provide great support when you have those moments of temptation. Of course, you also meet many new people and as a result, you can form new friendships which may just last a lifetime.

If you search online you'll also find many community groups which are formed of various people who practice this type of lifestyle. Again, these are valuable sources of information and inspiration, and great places to socialise. It goes without saying that you should always be careful about meeting someone in person when you've only talked to them online but provided you take the proper precautions, you'll find these community groups to be a fantastic way to link up with others who think and feel the same way that you do.

Minimalism is not something which only a few people practice. It's actually a growing way of life across the world. So many people have become frustrated with the constant consumerism battle that comes our way in the modern day, and as a result, they embrace a simpler life instead. We've talked about the benefits time and time again, and sharing your experiences with other people who might be considering minimalism is a great way to help them out too. You'll find the minimalist community to be very supportive, and a great way to meet people, learn new tips and help others at the same time.

Practising Minimalism Whilst Traveling

The first time you take to the road for a vacation or a travel adventure, minimalism will play a part. How? Packing!

By travelling in a more minimalistic way, you can save yourself a world of stress and hassle, and you can also save cash on excess luggage charges too! Almost all the travel guides rank this as their number 1 suggestion when deciding what you need to bring with you – As less as possible.

This basically means taking only what you need and multi-using everything else. For instance, you would take travel wash with you and make use of laundry facilities, rather than taking all the clothes you own! You would also take one coat, rather than two, etc. It's not difficult when you think about minimalism when travelling, and it's probably something you've done before in the past when trying not to travel quite so heavily. With a little practice, it can be done. The challenge comes when you are travelling with children, but by the time you start to travel with this minimalist mindset in place, you should be quite well practised and have a few tips already.

The minimalist lifestyle will also teach you to enjoy what you are seeing because it's not about the monetary value or the things you can buy. You will really appreciate the beaches you see, the landscapes you pass, and the experiences you have as a family, couple, group, etc. Travelling with the minimalist mindset really allows you to appreciate and open your eyes to the beauty and wonder of the world in a much deeper way. This is what author and world traveler Rolf Potts talks about in his famous book called "Vagabonding".

Practice the methods for banishing materialistic temptations you use when you're at home and don't have your head turned too much by shops and markets. Focus more on what you're seeing and the experiences you're having, and the time you spend in a new location for however long you're there. This will be wonderfully rewarding on so many levels.

Moving Away From Materialism, to Find Your Passions and Tribe to Bring Meaning to Your Life

We're almost at the end of our book now, and you should be feeling inspired and excited, to begin with your new minimalist lifestyle. That's the hope!

The final point we need to make is about finding meaning in your life and finding the people you belong with, i.e. your tribe. Minimalism will help you find that, and the contentment and ease will become addictive. Ironically, a lot of scientific research on this topic points to the fact that the lesser you reach out to find meaning in external stuff, the easier it will be to find it inside yourself. People forget that meaning is inherently non-materialistic. You'll have more meaning in your life because you're not always focusing on things to own, which in the end leaves you feeling empty and bereft. Focusing on experiences, people, and the way you feel on the inside will bring you far greater meaning than any phone ever could!

Socialising with other people who have the same minimalist mindset will also allow you to create a new social circle. You will find support in like-minded people, and when combined with those who you hold dear in your life already, will create an enriching and new part of your life which you would never have had before. Minimalism isn't just about decluttering your home and giving things away which you don't use, it's about changing your entire view on life, finding that meaning you might have been lacking previously, and being more positive as a result.

What We Have Learnt in this Chapter

This chapter has really been about giving you an insight into the potential issues you might face when you first embrace the minimalist lifestyle. Willpower will get you though the majority of them, and questioning why you are doing what you are doing will also help you out. Remember, you do not have to explain your choices to anyone, and if you have decided to change your mindset and shun consumerism and materialism, that is your choice entirely.

Conclusion

And there we have it! We're at the end of our book on minimalism. How do you feel now? Excited? Intrigued? Keen to get started?

Give it a go and you'll quickly begin to see how wonderful it will make you feel. Decluttering your home and your mind are the first starting points and from there you'll form the foundation on which to base your endeavours. Minimalism isn't going to happen overnight, even if you do declutter your home. You'll constantly need to question your motivation whenever you feel the need to buy something, for the first part of the time at least. You might experience that occasionally you find temptation coming your way, and you'll need to use willpower to push it away and focus on the more important things in life.

Put simply, minimalism will be a challenge at first, especially if you are someone who has always held material goods in high esteem and have been a victim of the hoarding frenzy of the millennials and social media. It will take some soul searching and you will need to be very clear in your mind in terms of why you're doing it, i.e. why you're deciding to embrace minimalism over everything else. If you can remember those things in the times when the devil on your shoulder decides to come calling, you'll be able to sidestep the majority of challenges. The more you do it, the easier it becomes, and soon you won't have those temptation moments at all!

Don't fall foul to those advertising campaigns which promise you the world if you buy their product –see through the façade of things. They are trying to sell you a product in exchange for profit because that's how their business stays afloat. You might like to think there is more care and positivity in it, but it's not the case - businesses need profits at the end of the day.

Remember, minimalism is an intention. It is a decision to do more with less, and you have to use that intention in every part of your life. You'll find it's not just about decluttering your home and avoiding buying new things, it's about focusing your time and attention on the things that really matter in life. It's about having more time to spend with the ones you love and the opportunities to be able to have experiences, rather than own things instead. Minimalism is also about clearing your life of anything which is toxic, or anything which doesn't serve you well. The end result will be a clearer view of everything, a sense of confidence, happiness, and contentment that no product ownership in the world could give you. Remember, true happiness comes from within and that is what minimalism will help you achieve. Please don't forget to leave a rating and review for this book on Audible if you liked it. That will mean a lot to me and other listeners as well. Have a great day!

CPSIA information can be obtained
at www.ICGtesting.com
Printed in the USA
BVHW062254230521
607981BV00003B/222

9 781008 962705